# The Xenophobe's Guide to The Spanish

## Drew Launay

ЯR

RAVETTE PUBLISHING

Published by Ravette Publishing Limited
P.O. Box 296
Horsham
West Sussex RH13 8FH
Telephone: (01403) 711443
Fax: (01403) 711554

First printed 1993
Revised 1994, 1996

Series Editor – Anne Tauté

Cover designer – Jim Wire
Printer – Cox & Wyman Ltd.
Producer – Oval Projects Ltd.


**An Oval Project**
for Ravette Publishing.

# Contents

'Andalusians, Aragonese, Basques, Castilians, Galicians, though feeling distinct from each other, feel a good deal more different from foreigners.'

The population of the Spanish is just over 39 million (compared with 48 million English, 57 million French, 57 million Italians and 80 million Germans).

# Nationalism and Identity

## Forewarned

The Spanish do not particularly care what other nations think of them, nor do they care about their country themselves. Such old patriotic sayings as 'The smoke of my native land shines more than the fire of others', or 'If God were not God he would be the King of Spain', have long been discarded.

When nationalism is enjoyable, the Spanish will be nationalistic, as they were with fervour for two weeks in 1992 during the Olympic Games in Barcelona.

Never having really cared a fig about sport before, it dawned on them that being cheered on by family and friends for running, skipping and jumping might be rather gratifying, so they bothered.

Pride in their country's achievements at football has been known to rise to the fore during a World Cup bonanza, but if Spain gets knocked out early they will switch allegiance at the drop of a sombrero to any country which has a player showing promise of zest and gusto. Usually a South American.

## How They See Others

The Spanish will only be aware of other nationalities if they have visited their country and had a great time.

Conversely, they will think little of them if they were bored there. As the majority of Spanish have failed to find any night life in Britain and cannot bring themselves to like the taste of flat, tepid bitter, they tend to ignore the English, regarding them as rather flat and tepid.

Brazilians they rate highly, however, as they never go to bed, and drink and dance the nights away.

The Spanish do not particularly differentiate between Austrians, Belgians, Chinese, Dutch, French, Germans, Italians or Japanese. All are *extranjeros* (foreigners), which is not a stigma, though they are often referred to by the risible name of '*guiri*' from the word *guirigay* meaning gibberish, the language most foreigners seem to speak.

Spaniards have an affinity with the *Sudacas* – South Americans – and, in sympathy with them, regard the North Americans as simple minded Fascists who should stay out of other people's countries and mind their own business.

Overall, however, they react to and judge the individual, not the horde, and what matters is whether people are amusing or not.


## How Others See Them

The Spanish are viewed as noisy, having no consideration for others, always late for appointments if they turn up at all, unreliable and never seeming to go to bed except in the afternoons.

Worst of all they appear indifferent to complaints, apparently capable of shrugging off any form of criticism.

Andalucía happens to be the biggest region, the hottest, the poorest; its people are the most vivacious, produce the most exciting dances, music and colourful costumes; so, for the holiday tour organisers, it has been promoted as the real Spain, but it would be hard to imagine an Andalusian and a Galician sitting at a table eating their bread dipped in olive oil and garlic and drinking their coffees while arguing that either one of them is more Spanish than the other.


## How They See Each Other

For the Spanish, the issue of nationalism tends to be confused by language.

In the 15th century when Isabel (the Castilian) and Fernando (the Arrogant) got married and there was a semblance of order and unification, *castellano*, the language spoken by Isabel, became the accepted form of communication. But as time passed, various areas decided they wanted to show independence and started talking in different tongues.

When Franco came along after the uncivil war, he tried to unify the country again by forbidding such nonsense. It only succeeded in driving these aspirations to autonomy underground. The moment he shuffled off his mortal coil, they all popped up, waving their own flags and screaming freedom.

In the Basque region, which they call Euskadia, the traffic indications are in Basque, they have their own Basque police force, raise and collect their own Basque taxes, run their own Basque schools, have their own Basque television channel, as well as their very own terrorist group ETA (*Euskadia Ta Askatasuna* = Euskadia and Freedom).

In Cataluña, with its capital Barcelona, they insist on speaking catalan and will be very rude to non-catalan speaking Spaniards who make the mistake of addressing them in *castellano*.

And in Galicia it's very nearly the same.

There are seventeen such regions in Spain, each with its

own capital, flag and legislature, many toying with the idea of speaking a different language. But as you travel South the sun thankfully gets hotter and enthusiasm for bringing out new dictionaries decreases as the siesta gets longer.

Andalusians, Aragonese, Basques, Castilians and Galicians, though feeling distinct from each other, feel a good deal more different from foreigners. That is as far as their nationalism goes. They are not patriotic. They will prefer to wave their separatist flags than the national flag because they like the different colours, but those people who demonstrate or discuss such feelings are politically orientated students or politically minded intellectuals, not the majority who are indifferent.

There is, however, one exception to this rule. Ask a Catalan if he is a nationalist or in any way patriotic and he will answer passionately in the affirmative. He will not, however, be referring to Spain as his country, but Cataluña.

## How They See Themselves

The Spanish, if they think about it at all which is doubt-ful, see themselves as totally acceptable people in a world where many are not.

# Character

Anyone attempting to understand the Spanish must first of all recognise the fact that they do not consider anything important except total enjoyment.

If it is not enjoyable it will be ignored.

Capable of finding boundless energy to satisfy this pleasure seeking, their enormous capacity for having fun results in any unexpected form of entertainment taking precedence over everything else.

Which means that they change their minds continually. Planning does not play any part in their lives.

All that is predictable about the Spanish is their unpredictability.

When visiting the country you cannot act upon the old dictum 'When in Spain do as the Spanish do', because no-one knows what they will be doing next.

*Individualismo* – self-reliance, which is at the root of the Spanish character results in a reluctance to sacrifice any part of their own interests to the common good. They therefore never suffer from guilt and are intolerant of criticism, although they will point out faults to other people's faces without apology.

The Spanish are not ambitious, envious, or easily impressed, and to any personal question they will probably only shrug their shoulders by way of suggesting that the answer is not important, e.g:

Q: What political party do you support?
A: A shrug of the shoulders.

Q: How many times have you been married?
A: A shrug of the shoulders.

Q: Would you like a beer or a coffee?
A: A shrug of the shoulders.

This attitude can sometimes become irritating when you ask a railway official the time of the next train for Madrid.

Time, of course is fundamentally immaterial to the Spanish because it suggests a limit to freedom, and a limit to freedom definitely suggests a curb on enjoyment.

The vital word to remember in their vocabulary is *mañana* (usually accompanied by a shrug of the shoulders) and this means 'Tomorrow', or 'Some time tomorrow' or 'The day after tomorrow', or 'The day after that', or 'Next week', 'The week after next', 'Next month', 'Maybe next month', 'Next year', 'Possibly next year', 'Best think in terms of the year 2000', 'Later', 'Sometime', 'Never', 'Never ever'.

# Behaviour

Rules for decent behaviour were laid down by the Church in post Civil War Spain and assiduously observed. Women were not to appear on the street with dresses which were too tight 'in those places which provoke the evil passions of men'; no woman was to be seen on a bicycle, or wearing trousers, and 'modern' dancing was strictly forbidden.

Ill-informed foreigners believe such attitudes still prevail. Not so. These days women appear in the streets with dresses so tight that the evil passions of men pop out of their eyes; unisex mountain bikes are ridden with a vengeance by aerobic buffs; females not only wear jeans but make sure that their silky suntanned skin can be seen through deliberate tears on the thighs, at the knees and across the bottom, and modern dancing has been replaced by spirited disco gyration.

# The Family

It could be said that the family governs the Spanish outlook on life, certainly their enjoyment of life. They will seldom plan anything, but when they do, they will consider members of the family within those plans or they will not feel happy.

An old Spanish folksong underlines this:

'You are not beautiful and you have no money but you love my mother and for that I love you.'

Family and home are much more important than material gain, and moving away from comfort and security is regarded as an indication of failure rather than achievement. In fact, mothers do not understand why their sons should want to to leave home for any other purpose than to start one of their own. Even then it is the wife who is expected to move away from her family, not him.

# Children

To the Spanish children, to whomsoever they belong, come first, and the banning of children from bars or places of adult entertainment, as practised in Britain, is not only unthinkable but looked upon as uncivilised.

Children should not only be seen but encouraged to be heard, loudly, for they are the evidence of life and continuity which must be heralded with joy. They are never sent to bed as a punishment, indeed they are never sent to bed at all. Many a toddler will be seen playing with a toy under a crowded café table at two in the morning, while the proud parents and friends admire the olive shaped eyes, the curly locks or the new disposable nappies.

# Elders

Behaviour towards the elderly is similarly exemplary.

It is unusual for the Spanish not to look after the aged members of their family.

Homes for geriatrics are few and far between, and only for the truly unfortunate who have no-one to take care of them. In most towns and villages grandfathers and grandmothers, great-grandfathers and great-grandmothers, will be seen sitting on the front doorstep or on a balcony in a rocking chair happily watching the world go by in the street, still belonging to the community, whether patriarchal, matriarchal, ga-ga or snoring.

# Eccentrics and Minorities

Spanish eccentrics are rather rare; no-one takes much notice of extraordinary behaviour since the days of the invading American hippies.

The admired eccentric is perhaps the old style Señor who rides a horse through the town with the arrogance of one who owns the place because he probably does, or the less liked, too smooth, young man who grows the nail of one of his little fingers half a centimetre longer than the others to make it plain that he is not a labourer, and to show disdain for those who are a *chulo* (pimp) or a *gitano* (gipsy).

The Spanish are not racist. They just hate gipsies with a passion and won't have anything to do with them if they can possibly help it.

Apart from this lack of civility towards these handsome and fierce looking people, they are generally unaware of the colour or creed of others as there is no reason why it should concern them.

# Manners

The Spanish generally tend to be less formal about manners than other nationalities. They will hope that their children will behave well in public, but not harangue them at home like the French. Elbows on the table will not be encouraged but will not deserve a slap.

"Sorry" and "Thank you" are not words you hear very often. Apologies for minor misdemeanours are not expected, nor is gratitude lavished on the generous. The Spanish deem such things artificial or false. If they are pleased they show it; similarly they make little effort to hide displeasure.

Knives and forks together to one side of the plate at the end of the meal is as customary as anywhere else. Table manners come second to gluttony. Enthusiasm for what is placed in the centre of the table will often have everyone immediately stretching across each other and using their fingers to get a mouthful, until someone puts everyone in order by kindly serving individual platefuls.

The sale of paper napkins (thrown on the floor under the table) has made millions for several clever business men.

In some families very old people still prefer to eat alone and in private. During the years of extreme poverty they developed a prudery about eating because it was considered a luxury, and each member prepared his own food and ate at a separate table with his back to the others.

## Greetings

Spain's social behaviour is probably the most informal in the world. Though the language provides for a courteous '*usted*' (you) and a familiar '*tú*' (you), on first being introduced, the '*usted*' is often dropped as no-one can be bothered with formality. For foreigners the question of which to use and when can be a problem, for '*usted*' said in a sarcastic tone can be insulting, suggesting that the person addressed is behaving arrogantly.

On the other hand old ladies cannot be addressed as '*tú*', nor can persons of importance, but to make the mistake of saying '*usted*' to a policeman on traffic duty in order to curry favour might land you with a parking fine though you may not even have a car.

To be addressed as *Don* or *Doña* in Spain is a mark of respect. Academics, doctors, lawyers and other professional people will be referred to as *Don* (Juan, Diego, Quixote) as it is a title for a gentleman or lady used only in front of the Christian name.

Spanish men have artfully established the tradition of kissing all women on both cheeks while shaking their hand. Introductions at home, in the street, in cafés, restaurants or wherever, therefore take longer than in France (where an hour should be given to shake the hands of everyone in sight) as men will kiss women, women will kiss women, children will kiss children, aunts will kiss uncles, cousins, grandfathers, grandmothers, the cook, the thief, his wife, her lover.

All this because, on the whole, the Spanish are emotionally demonstrative and gregarious. They love to meet new people, old people, old friends, new friends, and to this end continually make appointments for morning coffee, luncheon, afternoon coffee, dinner, late night coffee, late late night coffee.

# Etiquette

The fact that 98% of such appointments are not kept is due to etiquette. The Spanish consider it very rude to leave the company of whomsoever you are with before whomsoever you are with has finished telling you whatever it is they are telling you.

Since the Spanish are never in a hurry to finish anything, whatever they are telling you may take an hour or two, or three. As it is impolite to interrupt them to even let them know that you have another appointment, you don't, relaxed in the thought that whoever you were going to meet five hours ago will not be waiting impatiently at the appointed place because they too are listening to an endless saga from a friend they cannot interrupt and have missed three trains and two buses and will never make it either.

This total inability to keep appointments results in the happy certainty, in the minds of many married couples, that their partner cannot commit adultery because clandestine love affairs in Spain are an impossibility.

If a husband has booked a secret room for a quick rendezvous with his secretary after office hours on a Tuesday, knowing his wife is busy visiting a distant aunt, it is unlikely that the planned love affair will ever take place because:

1. He will meet an old schoolfriend on the way to the hotel and have coffee with him to talk over old days (three hours).

2. The secretary will be invited to have a coffee with another secretary to discuss the pros and cons of the planned affair (four hours).

3. The wife will not go to see the distant aunt because she's met a nice young man at the station who has suggested a coffee in the railway buffet and has told her he loves the shape of her body (two to three hours).

## Queuing

Queuing in shops could not be said to have been invented by the Spanish.

It is a matter of pride, which glints in wide eager eyes, to succeed in getting served first in any shop with as little subtlety as possible, resulting in *extranjeros* getting very hot under the collar at the butcher's unless they are themselves well versed in the art of queue-bashing.

Strong, sharp elbows and a good weight are an advantage; also some idea about the butcher's family problems on which you can give advice over the heads of everyone, in the loudest voice you can muster.

The butcher, or butcher's wife, or their apprentice, will be completely indifferent to the scuffling taking place on the other side of the counter, and will serve whoever comes into their line of vision first, or whoever has the most interesting piece of gossip.

To be armed with the rumour of a neighbour's recent adultery is a sure way of getting your pork chops before anyone else.

Sometimes a foreign female will find herself pushed to the fore by the locals and gratefully believe that they are showing polite respect for her comparative gentility.

Wrong. They just want her out of the shop so that they can have a good laugh at how ridiculous she looks in her straw hat.

# Beliefs and Values

## Wealth and Success

Though pride in possessions is not a national trait, to own a grand house, a flash car or valuable jewellery is important to the Spanish, but for personal enjoyment rather than one-upmanship. What the next door neighbours do with their wealth, if any, is entirely their business.

A new but not very serious snobbery is emerging within the nouveaux riches, based on all the obvious trappings of modern society. But snobbery as practised by the French and class as practised by the English do not exist. The Civil War was a great leveller.

The Spanish do not feel the need to strive for money in the northern European manner. They have always known that basic happiness is found within oneself and in one's natural surroundings: sun, contentment, security in nature.

The happiness of the individual is considered to be much more important than money. The goatherd who strolls the countryside with his animals breathing in the fresh air and loving his problem-less life is much more admired than the wealthy industrialist who hasn't time to *disfrutar la vida* (enjoy life) and spends quite a lot of his earnings on medicines to calm his peptic ulcers.

If the Spanish show off at all it is through noise, preferably at night to make sure that everyone is aware that they are alive. At one in the morning they will let you know they have hired a new set of videos or acquired a CD, turning the sound up to full volume, while in the streets mopeds will compete with souped-up Hondas. A well oiled engine can cause them anxiety; the sound of machinery at work is evidence that people are active.

Stillness is unsettling, which is why Spanish is not spoken but shouted, except between the hours of three and five in the afternoon when no-one talks because they are all asleep.

# Religion

Contrary to general belief, Spain is not a religious country. Roman Catholic it may be, but it is no longer religiously orientated except on saints' days which are celebrated with extravagant pageantry.

Whereas in the United Kingdom only three saints have managed to get their names permanently on the calendar (St. George, St. Andrew and St. Patrick), in Spain a dozen are remembered each month. Every province, every town and every village has its patron saint with his or her commemorative day – a glorious excuse for a fiesta.

There are as many male saints as female saints, but whereas the near life-size statues of the gentlemen paraded round the streets on feast days tend to be drab in brown, rust, grey or off-white robes, the ladies are glamorous in comparison. Often with tear-stained cheeks and pale but interesting complexions, they are invariably draped in sky blue or turquoise, with white embroidered veils, shimmering silver crowns on their heads surmounted by golden halos.

*Santos* and *santas* are all taken for a walk-about in procession some time during the day or night of their anniversary, on the backs of twelve strong men and true, often followed by the statues of Jesus Christ and the Virgin Mary.

People do not flock to church in thousands on Sundays, but tend to stand outside in the street watching the few elderly faithful come out, curious to see whether their expressions show signs of having gained anything worthwhile from any experience within.

As for the younger generation, they have to learn the Catechism by rote in order to take their First Holy Communion at the age of eight, but only so that the grandparents, parents, uncles, aunts, first cousin, second cousin, third cousin and all their families have an excuse for another fiesta, to which the priest hopes to be invited.

The history of Spanish religion unfortunately tends to go hand in glove with the image of cruelty, all because of the Inquisition.

Tomás de Torquemada (1420-1498) was the first Inquisitor General and he holds some respect in the minds of the Spanish for, though rather beastly to people who refused to believe in what he believed in, he was not dull and thoroughly enjoyed what he did.

Clearly he was not the only one for, after he died, the persecutions continued. Statistics show that the nation was drained of free thinkers between 1471 and 1781 at the rate of over 1,000 persons per annum. The actual figures for those three hundred odd years being 32,000 burnt at the stake, 17,000 burnt in effigy (those who unsportingly gave up the ghost in prison before they could be got to the barbecue), and 291,000 condemned to various innovative bits of torture.

The Church does not torture anybody any more, but looks to the Vatican to create lots of new saints so that more festive days, the alternative religious entertainment, can be added to the calendar.

# Custom and Tradition

## Strolling

The tradition of strolling about town to meet people in the evenings, known as *paseo*, is an old Spanish tradition as is its corollary, *ocio*, diversionary chatting. The Spanish will do this anywhere at any time.

Although the middle classes have become aware of the benefits of life away from the noise and pollution in larger cities, and can afford to live in the quieter and healthier surrounding countryside, their insatiable enthusiasm for meeting friends and their compulsion to walk the streets arm in arm to meet others walking the streets arm in arm, forbids them from moving too far from the centres.

Many of those who have tried out of town living have given up and returned to the hubbub, finding suburban life unbearably boring.

There is also the fear, away from town life, that they might be missing out on something new.

## Surnames and Christian Names

The use of a double-barrelled surname is traditional and needs a certain amount of concentration to understand it.

Women, on getting married, do not adopt their husband's surnames, they continue with their own. Children, on being born, are given their father's first surname first followed by their mother's first surname. Thus:

- If Felipe Rodríguez Fernández marries Pilar Gómez Díaz, her name will remain as Pilar Gómez Díaz.

- If they have a daughter christened Mercedes, she will be called Mercedes Rodríguez Gómez.

- If Mercedes Rodríguez Gómez marries Juan García Martínez, her name will continue to be Mercedes Rodríguez Gómez, but her son, Pedro, will be called Pedro García Rodríguez, and his sister Carmen will be called Carmen García Rodríguez.

Fortunately, in business only the first surname is used. Felipe Rodríguez Fernández will be known as Sr Rodríguez. On some official documents, to make sure that no mistakes are made, a woman will acknowledge her husband's name by admitting that she belongs to him. Thus Pilar Gómez Díaz having espoused Felipe Rodríguez Fernández, will sign herself Pilar Gómez Díaz de Rodríguez.

When poor Felipe dies, Pilar may well sign herself Pilar Gómez Díaz *viuda de* (widow of) Rodríguez.

All these double-barrelled names are never hyphenated except when they are double-barrelled names as exist in England, in which case the owner will have three surnames, for example, Fernando González Molina-Torres, Molina-Torres being the English-style double-barrelled surname.

And if both members of a married couple happen to have doubled-barrelled names then their offspring will have four surnames, e.g: Javier Aguilar-Pascual López-Matías.

In order to facilitate everyone's understanding of all this, tradition also has it that many sons are given the same Christian name as their fathers, and daughters the same Christian name as their mothers, so that in one family there may well be several Eduardos and several Margaritas who will invariably be called by their nicknames to confuse the issue even more, e.g: Francisco = Paco, José = Pepe, Manuel = Manolo, Enrique = Quique; María Isabel = Maribel, Providencia = Provi, Inmaculada = Inma, Remedios = Remi, Dolores = Loli, and so on.

It should also be noted that many boys are called José María, and many girls are called María José. So that if you have a father and son called José María and a mother and daughter called María José, it may be best not to invite them too often to tea.

Compared with looking up people in a Spanish telephone directory, all the above is kids' stuff. Phone numbers are listed under the surnames of the happy owner of the telephone.

Felipe Rodríguez Fernández will therefore be listed under Rodríguez Fernández, F.

Because he has many relatives with the same name, you are likely to find seven hundred odd Rodríguez Fernández, F. If you are unlucky enough not to know his address, then it is advisable to give up the attempt to contact him by phone. He will probably be out having a coffee anyway.

Should you need to ring a chemist or a plumber or a garage and you are clever enough to know that the chemist is known as Farmacia Pintada (because it is in a street called Calle Pintada) or that the plumber works with his brother under the name of Hermanos Moreno (the Brown Brothers) or that the garage you are seeking is a Renault garage, you will not be able to look them up under those names. Business telephone numbers are listed under the name of the person who pays the telephone bill – which in all probability will be the pharmacist's mother--in-law, the plumbing brothers' aunt, or the original owner of the land on which the Renault garage was built ten years ago.

# Birth, Marriage and Death

With television soap dramas from South America capturing the hearts and minds of mothers, grandmothers and great-grandmothers who normally look forward to a birth, a marriage or a death in the family to alleviate the tedium of daily life, babies, weddings and funerals have become less vital.

The nightly excitement of sitting down in front of the little screen to learn whether Manuela and her stepsister's niece are pregnant from the same wretched but beautiful lad about town, tends to upstage the normally longed for family gathering, though a great deal of time and energy and an even greater amount of money is still spent by the Spanish on clothes, cots, prams and toys for the newborn, not to mention the fortune poured out on a daughter's nuptials, or on an elaborate coffin for the dear departed.

The Spanish way of birth differs little from any other, except that the mother may be rushed off to hospital at the twelfth hour rather than the eleventh, due to much shrugging of shoulders on her part when she first feels the tell-tale paroxysms. This is because she is sure the event will not be enjoyable and prefers to delay it for as long as possible.

Many a child first sees the light of night in heavy traffic in the family car or a taxi on the way to the emergency ward and many more in a bus because the father-to-be is unavailable as he is out having a coffee with the taxi driver.

'Happy Birthdays' are celebrated twice a year, once on the anniversary of the actual birth and once (more importantly) on the child's saint's day, for it is unusual for anyone in Spain not to be named after a saint. This, of course, enables the parents to invite the grandparents, aunts, uncles, first cousins, second cousins, third cousins and their families to two fiestas per annum instead of one.

Weddings are the same as in any other part of Christendom, more attention being paid to the bride's gown and the uncle-with-video-camera weaving about at the altar than to the religious ceremony itself. Bridesmaids abound, confetti and rice are hurled around with abandon, bouquets are thrown over the shoulder for the next victim.

Funerals in Spain, however, are different and over very quickly. If there is no cold storage available for a corpse, it must be 'buried' within 72 hours. If there is cold storage available, no limit applies.

Cadavers are not buried but 'niched' in holes as granite tends to make the grave digger's job a trifle tiresome. Whole caskets are placed in large brick and cement holes and sealed up with more bricks and cement.

Niches are not usually purchased but rented from the council which runs the cemetery. If the rent is not paid the coffined remains are removed after a time and placed in a common grave site within the consecrated grounds to leave the niche free for another incumbent whose family will pay the rent.

The tradition of dressing in mourning is fast disappearing. Whereas in the past a wife, daughter or sister of the deceased was expected to wear black for years and, if they were unlucky enough to lose husband, father and brother consecutively, wear black for the rest of their lives, many a merry widow is now seen a month or two after the death of a spouse sporting bright clothes or a multi-coloured jump suit on her way to the aerobics class.

This is not meant to demonstrate a lack of feeling but simply a desire to get on with living life to the full as, after all, mourning is not enjoyable.

# Divorce

Since 1980 divorce in Spain has been easy-peasy.

If husband and wife agree to separate they can be divorced after two years.

If one of the couple doesn't want to separate then the other has to be cruel, leave home or commit adultery to obtain a legal separation five years after which a divorce is granted.

A husband wanting to rid himself of a nagging but clinging wife therefore has to beat her, pack his bags and go home to mother.

A woman wanting to drop a dull but dependent husband can kick him where it hurts, pack up her bags, or go off with the milkman. (However, milkmen as known in England do not exist in Spain as milk is not delivered to the doorstep.) Newspapers are not delivered either, so it's no use looking for a toy-boy.

Best bet is the knife grinder who pedals his grindstone round the streets on a bicycle, Thursday mornings.

# Culture

The Spanish respect culture. Culture for the more erudite is taken very seriously and the thirst for learning and open demonstration of intellectual prowess is admired. Far from being derisive to call a girl a 'blue stocking', it is very much a compliment.

To be appreciated by the Spanish you should swat up on the arts of Spain because if you encounter anyone with a milligram of intelligence, they will suss your ignorance about their culture very quickly.

You will not be expected to reel off the poems of Aleixandre, Alberti, Cernuda, Diego, Guillen or García Lorca, but if you did they would be flattered. What matters more to them is that you have an opinion on their works.

Probably the most quoted poem in the Spanish language, entitled *La cogida y la muerte* (The Tossing and the Death), is by Federico García Lorca who was shot by the nationalists during the Civil War for his romantic efforts.

It is a lament written after the death of the bullfighter Ignacio Sánchez Mejías, and epitomises all that is vitally important to the Spanish about death and glory.

At five in the afternoon,
It was exactly five in the afternoon,
A boy brought the white sheet
At five in the afternoon.
A frail of lime made ready
At five in the afternoon.
The rest was death and death alone
At five in the afternoon.

It goes on for another forty six lines, every other line repeating 'At five in the afternoon' and includes:

And a thigh with a desolate horn...
The bull alone exultant...
When the bullring was covered with iodine...
In the distance the gangrene now is coming,
A lily trumpet in his green groins.'

The other most quoted poem, or rather rhyme, was that chanted in whispers to the tune of the national anthem by schoolchildren when Franco was in power:

Franco, Franco
Has a white bum
Because his wife
Washes it with Ariel.

The rest of Spanish culture falls between these two offerings influenced in its infancy by Cervantes' *Don Quixote*, the lunatic exploits of the knight of the doleful countenance and his peasant side-kick Sancho Panza, a tale which though nearly four centuries old remains the most enjoyable.

It will not be enough to know that Cervantes or Pérez Galdós are the country's most popular classical writers, that Velázquez, Goya, Dalí, Miró and Picasso are its leading artists, de Falla, Granados and Rodrigo its best composers or that Calderón de la Barca, Agustín Moreto y Cavana, Tirso de Molina and Lope de Vega were its playwrights of the golden age. Children learn all that at school.

The international meditative intelligentsia discuss whether the novelists under Franco – Max Aub, Pío Baroja, Torrente Ballester, Camilo José Cela, Miguel Delibes or Luis Martín Santos – were more socially realistic than the post Franco writers: Juan Benet, Rosa Chacel, Antonio Gala, Muñoz Molina, Manuel Vázquez Montalbán or Terenci Moix.

Or whether the films of Almodóvar, Arillán, Berlanga, Buñuel, Camus, Vicente Erice, Pilar Miró or Carlos Saura gain prestige over imported films because these are seldom shown in their original version, a tradition left over from Franco who made the dubbing of foreign films compulsory so that they could be censored more easily.

One aspect of Anglo-Spanish culture which amuses as well as puzzles the Spanish is that the English, not being a nation of foreign language speakers, tend to read English authors on Spain, whereas the Spanish read English authors on the English.

In the majority of educated homes, a volume of Shakespeare's plays will sit beside perhaps a set of Dickens, probably Oscar Wilde, maybe Somerset Maugham and D. H. Lawrence.

The English, however, have gleaned the Spanish character from Robert Graves, George Orwell and Gerald Brenan (if not Ernest Hemingway) who were all weaned on the travel writer George Borrow, who was weaned on Richard Ford.

How many English homes, the Spanish ask, have a set of Benito Pérez Galdós on their shelves, or even Camilo José Cela?

## The Press

The Spanish are not avid newspaper readers. The papers with the largest circulation (all under 400,000) are *El País, El Mundo, ABC* and *La Vanguardia* and there is no demand for a tabloid press that dwells on the privacy of the Spanish royals or the misdemeanours of country priests.

Other periodicals publish heavy political articles together with nude centrefolds. Serious-minded businessmen, it has been admitted long ago, enjoy titillation while drinking their coffee.

## Song and Dance

The *cante jondo*, at least 400 years old, is a highly respected form of singing. *Cante jondo* buffs will not tolerate anyone thinking they can do it (since it sounds off key), or thinking it's just a matter of holding a note forever.

It is, in fact, off key, and the singer will hold a note for ever, but at the same time will cleverly tell you about love, sorrow, torment, honour, deceit, death, broken hearts, distress, misfortune, pain, regret, stress, solitude, travail, lamentation, trauma, calumny, apoplexy, catastrophe, the devaluation of the peseta, mother-in-law problems, despair, and grey hair.

When not singing passionately, the Spanish dance passionately: the *sevillana,* a complicated rhythmic but graceful dance exploring the love/hate relationship between a fiery couple from Sevilla (a few near kisses, near misses, lots of stamping of feet and if-looks-could-kill); the *flamenco,* an uncontrollable Sevillana, male and female competing to the death with their high heels; the *jota,* a merry hop, skip and jump, not unlike that performed by the Messrs Morris but without sticks or bells or straw hats; the *sardana,* Cataluña's haunting but repetitive circular dance; and the *fandango,* Andalucía's more lively version of the latter with much stamping of feet and castanets galore.

# Rock

Urban youth in Spain is not dissatisfied enough with life to create the right aggression for ordinary rock. But with the addition of the incessant rhythmic handclapping and wild strident vibrancy of flamenco singing, *rock-con-raíces* (root-rock) has emerged as a force to be reckoned with. It amply gratifies the Spanish need for exuberant and invigorating music.

Root-rock is therefore played, well or badly, but very loudly, at every possible fiesta, along with the inevitable show of folk dancing, the one guaranteed manifestation of culture propagated by village councils because they are always able to get a few locals to dance a jig and this will not cost the town hall more than a barrel of wine.

# Leisure and Pleasure

## Annual Holidays

The average family's idea of a holiday is to go to the beach, with all the paraphernalia available, at the crack of midday and stay there till sunset.

Loud cassettes are essential and a great deal of shouting and screaming helps the day along, mainly to let others know that they are having a great time. Portable barbecues are a must, as are enormous paella dishes and huge tents suitable for harbouring a family of twenty-two from vicious storms, which will never materialise.

Though camping is forbidden on many beaches, the law is totally ignored and no-one thinks of objecting, except the odd foreigner who believes, for some reason, that the beach belongs to him alone. He will be invited to join the fun, probably get drunk and in the end make more noise than anyone else.

Travel abroad has also become important to the Spanish because other continents offer new experiences and the cheaper package holidays are sampled by all and sundry.

One aged lady who sells sweets and small plastic toys from a tiny Granada kiosk which is ice cold with the winds in winter and oven hot in summer stated, after returning from two weeks up the Amazon, "It is worth being cooped up in here for twelve months if you can fly like a dove once a year."

# Public Holidays

Every day in the calendar is a saint's day so that some-where in Spain an essential fiesta will be celebrated. San Salustiano, San Buenaventura, San Saturnino will not be forgotten, nor will Santa Obdulia, Santa Bibiana or Santa Aurelia.

All essential services grind to a halt, everyone gets drunk, so if the village in celebration happens to be a key link between major cities, they too will not function.

No-one, of course, is ever quite sure when the saint's days are, so it is wise to think in terms of public holidays taking place from 1st August to 31st July the following year.


# Bullfighting

The Spanish are popularly supposed to be cruel to animals. This is not so.

A farmer may occasionally be seen hurling stones at the odd stray dog which is a nuisance on his avocado planta-tion, but to his own beast the Spaniard will always be kind.

The reputation for barbarity comes, of course, from the bullfight. The Spanish are not ashamed of their interest in the subject, but consider it natural. Their view is that, unlike the English who get their hounds to savage inno-cent foxes while they sit safely astride a horse, the Spaniard kills a massive and dangerous animal, bravely, by himself with a not so formidable sword.

It is considered such an art that the journalists who report on bullfights in the daily press are not sports writers, but bullfighting critics, and their columns are supervised by the *jefe de cultura*, the arts editor.

Kenneth Tynan, one of Britain's most respected drama critics, wrote of bullfighting: 'The corrida is a rite in which heroism and beauty, the great absentees of western Europe, may be seen happily and inextricably embraced.'

Admiral Nelson would not have agreed. When he saw a bullfight shortly before the battle of Trafalgar, he thought the goring of two toreros had seemed like poetic justice, the bloodthirstiness of the spectators had made him feel he would 'not have been displeased to see them tossed'.

Alexander Dumas, who fathered *The Three Musketeers* was so strongly moved by the bullfight, that he felt 'none of the revulsion I had been promised. I, who cannot bear to see the cook kill a chicken, could not tear my eyes away from the bull that had already slain three horses and sorely wounded a human being.'

When attending a *corrida* you should take along a white handkerchief and a very dark pair of sunglasses.

The white handkerchief is to wave along with the cheering multitude to show appreciation at the kill and help the matador win the award of a much coveted ear, two ears or a tail.

The President of the fight, usually the local mayor or political dignitary, awards the appendages depending on the sea of white handkerchiefs he sees before his eyes. The pair of very dark sunglasses is to wear when said ear, two ears or tail are severed from the animal's carcass. Not a sight for the sensitive.

The thing to remember is that the fighting bull has spent his whole life being trained to kill man, cannot wait to get his sharp horns into the buttocks of the individual prancing about in front of him waving a red cape and dressed in a 'suit of lights', and has the option to survive by refusing to fight – which many bulls do.

It is believed that most bulls deem death to be a happy release from the fearful *paso-dobles* played incessantly throughout the fight by the local brass band.

But let Ernest Hemingway, as the self-appointed world aficionado on the subject, have the last word: 'The bull-fight has not existed because of foreigners and tourists, and any steps to modify it to secure their approval is a step towards complete suppression.'

Suppression is something the Spanish will not entertain.

# Fireworks

The Spanish cult of fire and noise is legendary and the profession of pyrotechnic is highly profitable if you can live with the fear.

The Valencia annual celebration of *fallas* (bonfire) during which some 76,000 kilos of fireworks are lit and exploded cannot, it is said, 'finish without thunder'.

All year the *falleros*, or bonfire makers, work on papier maché figures satirising the events and people who have made headlines in the previous twelve months, only for these giant figures, often rising three storeys high, to be hoisted into position on the day of the festival, and burned to the ground.

Accidents occur every time, and people get hurt, but this is considered to be part of the fun – so much so, that in the nearby town of Paterna they have perfected the art of the *corda*. Here a tightly packed crowd of people (dressed in several layers of clothes, wearing masks made of net, and heavy boots) let off 35,000 rockets in 25 minutes in the main street.

# Driving

Driving in Spain is hazardous.

There are several reasons for this, the main one being that the Spanish consider driving enjoyable and get behind the wheel with the same terrifying enthusiasm as a six year-old on his first solo bumper car ride at the fair.

Under Franco not many families had cars. In the cities and large towns people used public transport or walked, and in the country they used mules or the horse and cart. The mules were then replaced by motorbikes, the car industry was developed and everyone bought a van or a limousine in a very short space of time. Sixty year-olds who had never driven in their lives started cruising around in expensive Mercedes and Audis, while the younger generation bought turbo-driven Renaults with thundering sound systems for blaring out pop.

All were in such a hurry to speed down the new motorways with which the government quickly networked the country (the major roads are a delight) that they did not bother to apply for licences let alone pass a driving test or take out insurance. In small towns and villages where policing is more informal than in the cities, it is likely that only half the population drive legally.

During major holidays, when whole townships get in their cars to visit other townships, the death toll on the roads is horrendous, and the most vulnerable in such traffic are the northern European tourists who, having well disciplined and ordered minds, cannot believe that anyone will actually disobey the rules of the road through ignorance or lack of concentration.

The Germans and the French top the list for getting involved in accidents because they wrongly assume that other people will actually stop at a red light, or turn left when they have signalled that it is their intention to do so.

The British, ever considerate, weigh up the options offered to the driver in front more carefully and have fewer crashes.

A white line down the middle of the road which forbids overtaking is no guarantee that you will not be passed by twenty lunatic individuals hell bent on proving that their Seat Panda is as fast as the Swiss registered Lamborghini which just whooshed past you over the speed limit.

Zebra crossings are not the prerogative of pedestrians, but only an indication that the local council is aware that elderly people might want to get to the other side of the street, and that they have put some effort into thoughtfully providing a way for them to let drivers know of such desires. Zebra crossings are for pedestrians to wait on until drivers *allow* them to cross. At no time does any sane Spaniard use them, having learned by experience that the very sight of an authoritative sign to a driver will incite instant disobedience.

It should also be noted that pedestrians in Spain are as much a hazard as the drivers, because of the Spanish contempt for danger. On stepping off the kerb, the Spanish pedestrian, male, female, child or geriatric, will instantly see a snorting bull coming at them instead of a Peugeot 204.

With the swiftness of a practised *torero*, they will dart out in front of the oncoming vehicle, twirling like a crazed *banderillero* (the one who sticks barbs into the bull) arriving safely on the other side oblivious to the fact that they have caused several head-on collisions.

When the law regarding the wearing of seat belts and crash helmets came into force, for two whole weeks every motor cyclist in town was seen sporting a brand new helmet and car drivers clunk-clicked on getting in behind the wheel. It was a new fun thing to do.

Seat belts, however, soon proved tiresome, especially after a good coffee and doughnut, and helmets caused enormous confusion. Suddenly Paco realised that even his own mother did not recognise him as he roared past on his Vespa, and friends no longer waved at him, or worse, they recognised him too late causing him to turn round to acknowledge the greeting and crash straight into the back of the car in front (which had braked unexpectedly to avoid killing a twelve year-old matador).

Worse, Soledad who had bought a hibiscus pink helmet, and Concepción who had bought a lavender blue one, decided to swap because the colours didn't match their dresses, so everyone waved at the wrong person, causing more confusion and accidents.

But now all is under control. No-one bothers to wear a seat belt or a crash helmet. They are not enjoyable.

If you wish to survive as a driver in Spain, ignore the highway code and rely on basic instincts.

If you wish to survive as a pedestrian, don't walk.


## Television and Radio

The Spanish come second to the English with the highest television viewing figures in Europe. Almost every home has a set. Even in Andalucía with its hot summers, families purchase a television set before a refrigerator – they are more fun to watch.

Though nine channels transmit programmes, most areas only get the choice of five. The Spanish versions of American panel games and chat shows are the most popular.

Television news, both home and abroad, is comprehensive and upbeat with regular items about the arts – say, ballet or opera – forming an integral part of it.

Newscasters, both male and female, are attractive and usually optimistic about the eventual outcome of even bad events.

North and South American soaps, familiarly referred to as *culebrones* (giant snakes or serpents), and American, British and Spanish sitcoms, are all interrupted by countless motor car commercials which sell their products on high speed and power, thrilling the viewer with the danger they can experience if they sit behind the wheel.

Since there is nothing clandestine about the appreciation of sex, there is no censorship on normal television. Couples coupling merrily can therefore be seen by all ages at any time of the day or night, resulting in youngsters yawning with deep boredom during an otherwise dramatic film, while their parents turn up the volume on yelps of pleasure, heavy breathing and murmurations.

The times at which the programmes are shown, though published in the daily press, differ from newspaper to newspaper and often do not tally with what is seen on the screen. Because the evening news is scheduled for 10 p.m. and announced as such, it does not mean that it will be transmitted at 10 o'clock. Sometimes the newscasters will appear on screen at 10.05, or 10.10, or even 15 minutes later, depending on the length of the story their friend has been telling them over coffee in the canteen.

Some programmes are delayed an hour with no apology or explanation. Others never appear at all which guarantees that 3 million disappointed people throughout the country will shrug their shoulders more or less in unison.

Spanish radio pulsates rapid voluble talk and root-rock throughout the day from Madrid or local stations. At no time is an hour of relaxing music guaranteed, not even during the siesta when the disk jockeys will switch to an auto pilot programme of pop while they stick their ear plugs in and go to sleep.

# Sex

In Spain lust is ever in the air.

There is nothing about the Spanish appreciation of sex that is inhibited or restrained. It is accepted that both men and women love making love, which is why there are very few sexual crimes in the country. The pervert is usually a puritan who has been warned since childhood against the most serious sins of the flesh, or else he was educated in an English public school.

The Spanish let off sexual steam all their lives because they need to do so, and society finds it a normal and logical thing to do. It is very enjoyable.

The Church is no longer allowed to dampen people's enjoyment of sex; all edicts from Rome are ignored, and in many out of the way villages where the 20th century has not quite caught up, the people encourage their priest to have a mistress so that they can have peace of mind when their daughters go to confession.

The custom of *piropear* (saying flirtatious things) is an ideal opening gambit for the older and more gracious Spanish *caballero* (gentleman). All Spanish women know how to receive compliments gracefully, and all Spanish men are experts at paying them. Flattery, everyone knows, gets you where you want to go. To *piropo* (flirt) is the simplest way of letting a female know she is attractive; it has a wide range of shadings, and is gallantly used when describing aloud a woman's effect on a man, for example: 'Your throat, my girl, is so lovely and bright that the water you drink is seen through it...'

The younger Spaniard may well dispense with such eloquence, however, and use the more direct wolf whistle. Until he falls truly in love, he will have a tendency to assert his masculinity, deny that he can be sentimental, and calculate the minimum time he needs to be with a female, as did Don Juan Tenorio:

One day for winning her heart.
Another for bedding her.
One for leaving her.
An hour to forget her.
Two days to replace her.

The sight of an unusually exposed Spanish girl will exhilarate him, but he will quite likely shout "If you're not selling it, cover it up!" Though not to a foreigner.

On the other hand, Spanish girls are generally to be protected and kept innocent for as long as possible, while foreign girls are regarded as easy prey.

The English head the top of the list, possibly because there are more of them than Americans who come a close second. The Germans take the whole business a bit too seriously, the Scandinavians are clinical, the French tend to talk too much and compare performances, while Brazilians, Argentinians, Colombians and other South Americans are considered best, knowing how to make the conquest difficult with a promise of victory at the end, but only because they are far from home.

From the Spanish female point of view, the foreign male has little to offer that she can't find at home as far as sensuality is concerned, so non-physical attributes (humour, joie-de-vivre, money) can sway the balance.

Though loud car horns, motor cycles revving up, jack hammers hammering, chainsaws screaming and incessant shouting are not usually noises noticed by the Spanish, people will pause to listen attentively in empty night streets to the sensitive sound of a couple in climax from beyond a balcony and half open shutters.

# Eating

As the Spanish avoid thinking about time, and never plan, it is anybody's guess when meals will be served.

If you are a foreigner and inadvisably decide to throw a dinner party, invite your Spanish guests to come two hours before the time you plan to serve the meal.

Avoid delicate hot dishes, in fact avoid hot dishes altogether because, should they arrive at the appointed hour, they will talk for ever about how they managed it and ignore the food put in front of them.

The Spanish sense of urgency, or rather the total lack of it, affects everyone's eating habits, and any head waiter will tell you that the reservation of a table means nothing to him until the people are actually sitting down with their napkins unfurled.

Chefs in Spain never expect to stop cooking till 3 o'clock in the morning.

The inability to be punctual is the reason why the *paella* is the Spanish national dish. Rice and ancient country recipes dating back to the occupation of the Moors have nothing to do with it. The *paella* is a godsend to Spain for the ingredients can be prepared well in advance and be put aside till the guests arrive, then cooked for the essential twenty minutes while *gazpacho* (cold tomato, onion, cucumber, bread, olive oil and garlic soup) is consumed – keeping everyone happy.

The mixture of fried chicken, boiled fish, damp squid, uncooked prawns, tomatoes, peas, red peppers, green peppers, old boot laces, saffron and rice, guarantees that no-one can possibly know what it is supposed to taste like, so if it is undercooked or overcooked, no-one will complain.

The Spanish palate, compared with the French or Italian, generally makes simple demands.

The Spanish consume vast quantities of fried fish, grilled prawns, barbecued pork, raw cured mountain ham, fried squid, grilled sardines, barbecued chicken, raw cured mountain ham, fried pimientos, grilled anchovies, barbecued baby octopus and raw cured mountain ham, without sauces which are not particularly popular.

Average meals at home start the day with a freshly baked bread dipped in olive oil and stabbed with pieces of chopped garlic and black coffee – sometimes laced with brandy or aniseed, the children eating *churros*, a Yorkshire pudding-like dough sausage dipped in thick hot chocolate.

For lunch (which is never served before 3 p.m.) it will be *paella* or chips. Chips (*patatas fritas*) vie with *paella* as the national dish because the potatoes can be prepared in advance and just plopped into boiling olive oil when people declare themselves hungry. *Patatas fritas* are served with absolutely everything, including *paella*.

For dinner (which is never served before 10 p.m.), see lunch.

*Tapas* are the Spanish answer to all eating problems: a multitude of different snacks on offer all day in most bars, from olives to egg mayonnaise, pickled anchovies to Russian salad, hot sausages to bits of fried goat.

The majority of city workers no longer eat meals, but sit at bars sampling *tapas* with iced beer. This results in their coming home at night with little appetite, saving the housewife the effort of dropping the ready prepared *patatas fritas* in the boiling oil, which she does not much feel like doing as she had a *tapa* or two with an iced beer when she met her friend out shopping and has also lost her appetite.

# Eating Out

Visiting restaurants is not considered that much of a treat unless you are with a large party of friends or with a family group.

Choosing what to eat, which is definitely part of the fun, takes so long that the head waiter wisely places a large dish of raw cured ham and *manchego* cheese from la Mancha for the guests to chew on while they study the menu.

If the family are lunching out, father or grandfather will direct proceedings and take orders as best he can. Because he fancies prawns lightly fried in olive oil garnished with garlic and red peppers for starters, he will order it for everyone, only to be contradicted by his wife who will insist that their five, or ten, children should have garlic soup with grapes, while his sister-in-law and her husband will plump for a salad of courgettes, tomatoes, pimientos, and tuna laced with olive oil and garlic.

Fancying fish, Papa will then order *chanquetes*, tiny whitebait-like fish lightly fried in oil, a dish which is forbidden by law in Spain for ecological reasons, but is served in most restaurants and often seen consumed by high ranking Guardia Civil officers and Cabinet Ministers.

Three of his daughters who worry about such things will object and select three-tiered omelettes with tomatoes, potatoes, cured ham – cooked in olive oil and garnished with garlic – while Grandpapa, who shouldn't because his teeth are giving him trouble, will ask for baked bulls' testicle pie just to annoy the same three ecologically minded daughters.

Grandma will order partridges cooked in a rich chocolate sauce, laced with olive oil and garlic, because she hasn't had that traditional dish since just after the Civil

War, while her grandsons, who want to get the meal over quickly so that they can go out and play, will choose egg and chips and be given black pudding fried in olive oil and garlic served with pumpkin fried in olive oil with more garlic because their aunt wants to taste it but has decided on fried basted mussels garnished with mayonnaise, olive oil and garlic.

Red wine, white wine, beer, fizzy orange, fizzy lemonade and Coca-Cola will be ordered to wash all this down, and to round off the meal, everyone changing their minds and swapping over plates during the consumption of this feast, desserts will be chosen, more than likely flans all round, to make things easy.

Father might have an apple flan, Mother a coconut flan, five children condensed milk flans, Grandpa an orange flan, Grandma a pear flan, the boys a semolina flan, whether they like it or not, and the remaining uncles and in-laws vanilla flans. Olive oil and garlic optional.


# Drinking

The Spanish do not drink to release their inhibitions, as they have none. They drink because they are thirsty or wish to get drunk.

Drinking starts at about 2 a.m. and goes on in most discos and night clubs till well past the opening of office hours – 10.30 a.m.

Iced beer is the great favourite, gin and tonic, cold white wine, iced red wine. Sherry is drunk less than might be expected, brandies are good for cleaning paint brushes, *anís* (both sweet and dry) burns away indigestion. *Sangría* is reserved for tourists and is prepared from the dregs of all the half empty glasses left over from the night before.

# What is Sold Where

Spanish shopping times confuse visitors. Shops, however, can more or less be relied on to open between 10 a.m. and 2 p.m., then from 5 p.m. till 8 or 9 or midnight, depending on the city, town, *pueblo* (village) or shop-keeper's love life.

Stores in cities open all day, the management having apparently worked out an amazing rota system for their staff's siestas.

The giant supermarket is relatively new and a visit to one is still regarded by many as a form of entertainment. People tend to stare in awe at the million multi-coloured mountain bikes hanging from the girders above the plastic garden sun lounge display, feel absolutely no need to purchase anything, but may eventually be tempted to buy a box of cheese biscuits if it's on offer.

Other shops sell everything.

Though they may originally open with the intention of specialising in shoes, the owner will be tempted one day to sell a few of the eggs which her chickens have laid, after which there is no going back. Butchers sell fish, fish-mongers sell dairy products, dairies sell bread, bakers sell T-shirts, boutiques sell chewing gum, stationers sell vegetables.

Because of this, shopping is hazardous as no-one can tell you where it is best to get what or where the price is right. Most housewives shop at their cousin's or at their neighbour's uncle's sister's aunt's so that they know where to complain if the battery for the torch they never use doesn't work.

# Health and Hygiene

Some Spaniards like visiting the doctor, others fear doing so. Most haven't the faintest idea what they are suffering from when in pain, even when told, and rely on the medicine man's esoteric knowledge to be cured, or a neighbour's advice.

Chemists know their job and will diagnose the trouble from the description of discomfort given. They will prescribe a pill or three with suggested alternatives; if this doesn't work they will happily try something else till the patient has recovered – or died.

Spanish pharmacists mean well.

Hospitals are run like holiday hotels and at no time is anyone allowed to complain of feeling ill for too long. The nurses and doctors have never got over the fun of their student days and cavort around the place ceaselessly laughing at major blunders made by their colleagues or at terribly rude jokes.

Trolleys bearing patients who are at death's door are wheeled from intensive care wards to operation theatre as though taking part in the Monte Carlo rally, but any poor individual who is brought in after a motor accident and is known to have been the cause because of careless driving or drinking will not be treated kindly at all.

## Hygiene

Since the advent of television advertising, with nubile models showing everything to promote motor vehicles, insurance and condoms, women shave under the arms and everyone brushes their teeth regularly. The bidet is a standard fitting in any new bathroom, with revolving taps that squirt water in all possible directions.

The average family bathroom cupboard is much the same as any other, except that condoms are unlikely to be hidden away. Children using them as balloons is thought natural and funny.

The Spanish woman is broom mad and will sweep anything anywhere into a dustpan at all times of the day, often interrupting a conversation or even a phone call to collect a speck of dust or crumb perceived in a corner where it should not be.

The mop was probably invented specifically for Spain and brought into being by some astute Moor the moment the Alhambra floors were tiled, ever since which time no Spanish housewife worth her detergent powders is ever likely to be seen without one and a bucket to match. Even rugs are sluiced (and put out to dry), as are wooden floors, the interior of saloon cars and the bit of pavement in the street in front of the house.

In Andalucía the whitewashing of already shining bright white houses is an essential part of life. The sight of a grey patch on a façade, unless dealt with promptly, can cause cardiac arrest.

# Sense of Humour

The main thrust of Spanish humour comes from their attitude to danger.

People getting themselves in a tight spot and suffering the consequences, sometimes fatally, is found terrifically amusing. Hence the success of the annual fiesta when bulls are let loose in the streets of Pamplona to toss any individual with illusions of becoming a torero who misjudges the distance, a suicidal revelry repeated in many other towns for the sheer fun of the risk of being gored.

Similarly, a display of fireworks which goes wrong is invariably looked upon with some hilarity.

The Spanish love the English sense of humour and their ability to laugh at themselves without losing face. They appreciate sarcasm though seldom practise it.

Sex is considered the funniest human endeavour, and raunchy jokes will be told in front of anyone and on family television shows, children all ears, the adults accepting the fact that the exchange of such humour is rife at school anyway.

Black humour about the less fortunate is equally popular.

Not much interested in other nations, the Spanish do not go outside their own country to hurl insults. Jokes about mean people equivalent to English standard Scots jokes are invariably told about the Catalans who are supposedly meaner. The Catalans, of course, say that the Aragonese are far worse.

But the main recipients of the butt are usually a small number of people from a village called Lepe in the south west of Andalucía. Thus, the riddle: 'How many Irish, Belgians, Californians or whomever, does it take to unscrew a light bulb?' Answer: 'Four. One to hold the bulb and three to turn the chair' will be asked as 'How many people from Lepe...?'

Their reputation for being dim was supposedly acquired when a school inspector from Madrid asked the brightest student of the brightest class in the only school "Who stole the Rock of Gibraltar from the Spanish?" and got the answer "Not I, Sir." Repeating this poor example of learning to the headmaster, he was assured that if the boy had said he had not stolen the Rock, then it was certain he had not, as he was a very honest individual.

The Lepes, however, are not that stupid. Their mayor has cashed in on their reputation by inviting tourists to visit the town to experience Lepe oafishness for themselves.

# Crime and Punishment

The Spanish take little heed of any rules or regulations – they are not enjoyable. But with their passion for freedom they find the idea of imprisonment so abhorrent that they will keep a weather-eye open for the law enforcement officers, of which there are several kinds.

The *Guardia Civil* wear avocado green uniforms and used to wear black patent leather comic opera hats, but now sport soft peaked caps. They control the frontiers and patrol the countryside, highways and byways in cars, landrovers, on horseback, sometimes on donkeys, or on foot. All look fierce and their bark is as bad as their bite.

The *Policía Nacional,* who dress in hazelnut brown uniforms, control the population in towns of more than 20,000 inhabitants, are as highly strung as any other urban policemen, and blow their tin whistles incessantly.

The *Cuerpo Superior*, or super corps, are never seen because they go around in plain clothes. They are part of the *Policía Nacional* and do the sort of things the CID do in England.

The *Grupo Español de Operaciones*, the equivalent of the SAS, keep a very low profile until they are called upon to be heavy handed with the likes of terrorists, hijackers, kidnappers or bank raiders.

The *Policía Municipal* wear midnight blue uniforms with checkered bands round their chauffeur's caps and mainly shrug their shoulders at the misdemeanours of the inhabitants of towns with a population of between 5,000 and 19,999.

As the mayor is their paymaster, they will fine you for parking in the right or the wrong place if the local council is short of funds. You may ask them the way to the nearest petrol station, but they probably won't know. They may, however, cadge a cigarette off you.

All Spanish laws are easily run foul of as they seem to be invented on the spur of the moment to line the pocket of someone in authority. Law and corruption go hand in glove.

If in trouble it is best to seek the services of an *abogado* (lawyer, advocate, barrister) who will act on your behalf like an English solicitor. An *abogado* will also deal with all documents relating to the purchase or sale of properties, last wills and testaments, divorces, etc.

A *notario* (notary public) will also become involved as the officially appointed official to attest deeds, draw up contracts and administer oaths.

Delays on all levels are inevitable within the Spanish legal system so the best lawyer to get is not one with an astute mind, but the cousin of the little town clerk who arranges the court hearings and knows where he and his colleagues have their coffee.

## Prisons

In most cases the police can detain you and lock you up in a prison cell for up to 72 hours if they decide they don't like the way you are comporting yourself. After this passage of time you are given a chance to appeal against the arrest.

The *mañana* syndrome should be taken into account when calculating your release. Best think in terms of 72 weeks.

Prisons are not as terrible as might be expected. A middle aged Briton and Costa del Sol crook released from a Málaga prison, who had previously done time in an English jail, eulogized about his treatment by the Spanish authorities.

According to him, stress was greatly reduced by inmates being locked up in their cells for only two hours during the day, siesta times, and at night to sleep. Only two inmates occupied each cell which were fitted with washbasin and lavatory. Three out of every five cells had a television set, generously left behind by previous occupants.

Communication between prisoners and their families was encouraged. Private rooms were available for wives and husbands to spend two hours together once a week. Telephones were always available to ring family or lawyers. There were no prison uniforms, inmates could wear what they wished.

Prisoners were treated with respect and dignity at all times. Guards and prisoners could play board games together which led to an informal and relaxed atmosphere. Self-education was encouraged with computer courses provided. Every prisoner was allowed the equivalent of £40 per week of his own personal money to buy anything he wished except alcohol.

Shower and laundry facilities were available at any time, with a free supply of soaps and detergents, the standard of hygiene being very high. The food provided was wholesome and plentiful, allowing for various religious diets if requested. Medical care was thorough.

So, clearly, if you are a criminal, get caught in Torremolinos not Weston-Super-Mare.

# Brothels

Brothels are illegal in Spain, which does not, of course, mean that they do not exist. On the contrary, local authorities have long ago realised that brothels are a good thing to have around. They not only keep the male councillors happy, but boost tourism and help assuage the fiery passions of the younger men.

Brothels in most towns are signposted as a club, massage parlour or sauna. Those who object strongly to having a brothel in their neighbourhood can denounce the owner and report the unlawful activities to the police. They in turn will raid the offending establishment, discover that there are more beds on the premises than are usually necessary for a bar or discotheque, and suggest they are removed forthwith.

The following day great show will be made of loading them on to open lorries. The lorries will drive once round the town and take them straight back. The same night, it is business as usual.

The only setback will be to the person who reported the offence. Next time he or she needs the services of the plumber, carpenter, television engineer or fire brigade, they will find it inconvenient to call – till *mañana*.

A Moroccan lady of leisure who made a fortune in a house of pleasure revealed that the usual time allotted was seven minutes, the average age of the clients was 22 (mostly young conscripts away from home), that middle aged men were rare, and 60 year-olds a problem because they liked to gossip and took too long undressing.

For those who want to spend more than seven minutes on sexual appreciation, pornographic videos are freely available in most hotels and bars and in most apartment blocks at a specified hour once or twice a week.

The head porters who pipe video films all day to the

inhabitants of the flats choose the porn offerings, and after dinner on the chosen nights it is not unusual for a family, or couples with friends, or lonely hearts to sit in front of their sets and watch unimaginable goings-on between buxom German or voluptuous Scandinavian females and amazingly well armed adonises. In bright technicolour, mainly pink, all positions will be attempted.

Two elderly men from the *campo* (countryside) who, after a heavy day's work picking olives, happened to be in a bar one evening where such a programme was being shown, admitted surprise at what was going on.

"I had no idea you could do that to them" said one to the other. "I had no idea they did such things to you," retorted his companion.

"It's too late for either of us to try now," both sighed, ordering a bottle of cognac to drown their sorrows.

# Obsessions

## The Siesta

The siesta is undoubtedly the major Spanish obsession. Two hours' sleep after lunch is so sacred that anyone seen on their feet between the hours of 3.00 and 5.00 p.m. is considered insane.

## The Lottery

Gambling is a Spanish passion and the big gamble of the year is known as '*el gordo*', the Fat One. This takes place every 22 December and is reputed to be the biggest in the world.

The winning number pays out 300 million pesetas (approximately £1,500,000, but each ticket costs 30,000 pesetas (£150), so individuals usually buy a *décimo* (a tenth of a ticket), then organise groups in their clubs or offices to buy the whole.

The draw is an event of national importance watched by millions on television, when the orphans of the San Ildefonso school in Madrid pluck balls in relays out of giant revolving Bingo baskets and chant the numbers as though singing a psalm. The tradition is two centuries old and nearly as religious an occasion as the Christmas midnight mass.

## The Macho

The Spanish male, it is said, was not taught to be happy but to be a real (masculine) man. This might once have been true, but as no-one was able to define exactly what a real man was, the feminist movement had an easy time of it in Spain as soon as the population started taking notice of television advertising. Moving into key executive positions in the publicity world they got 'real' men to wash up the dishes, iron their own trousers and change babies' nappies.

To those Spanish men who still have any inclination to being macho, the sociologist José Vincent Marqués has an answer: 'If you want to be loved and obeyed, get a dog. If you like being right, get a parrot. If you're looking for arguments and live in a ground floor flat, get a mule.'

Machoism is not a Spanish obsession but a foreign obsession, about the Spanish male.

# Systems

As a rule, systems are not expected to work in Spain.

If a train runs on time it is a surprise and a bonus. If a plumber turns up when he said he would, it is astonishing; if a public telephone accepts the coins the first time, it is nearly a miracle, and if you get through to the number you dialled you must be on fantasy island.

When systems do work, however, the public are not particularly co-operative, especially when it comes to refuse collection.

## Rubbish

In the majority of Spanish towns and villages rubbish is supposed to be deposited at certain street corners and collected every day by the local council's dustmen, usually at dawn. This system works.

The refuse collectors are well equipped with up-to-date waste disposal units on wheels which noisily consume everything on the spot, waking everyone in the process, after which street cleaners come with brooms and water and mop the place up. Thus every day can be said to start with a clean bill of health.

What does not work is the Spanish attitude to rubbish. They dump refuse anywhere, at any time of the day, that is convenient to them. Having got rid of it, it is no longer their problem.

In the country even the authority's attitude is the same. Travel across Spain and your eyes will alight on blue plastic, orange plastic, black plastic, dog-worried bags along highways and byways, scattered by the winds. Old gas cookers, rusty refrigerators, twisted prams, bicycle frames and countless shattered television sets will be dumped along with used cars, discarded steam engines, oxidised olive presses, perforated water tanks, blown safes, false teeth and other non-biodegradable dross.

## Post

The Spanish postal system is another service which would work better if the public were more interested, but sending and receiving letters has just never been part of traditional life and advertisers are only just getting into their stride with junk mail.

The main problem with deliveries, should you ask a postman, is that houses in the pueblos do not have letter boxes. The inhabitants receive so little mail that letters are usually slipped under the door or thrown through an open window, sometimes to land on the tiled floor and slide under the favourite front room piece of furniture where it might lie for weeks unnoticed.

If the postman has a backache and a window is not open, he may not stoop till the next day. Private 'poste restante' lock-up niches have to be rented in the local post office if you really want to receive all your bills.

## Education

General education in Spain is run on similar lines to the French, that is the lycée – but with a difference. Whereas the French child will be severely reprimanded if he is late for school, or does not do the huge amounts of homework with which his satchel is laden every evening, if the Spanish child is late for school, which he usually is, he may still be in his classroom before the master.

In a television documentary on education a boy of twelve was interviewed on his daily routine and school discipline. He started explaining his day with "I usually get to school at 9 ... or 9.30 ..." The interviewer made no comment at all on this. It was acceptable and normal.

Children go to kindergarten at five, and start the lycée at six. They go through 8 grades which takes them to the age of 14 when, depending on their capabilities, they either go on to the *formación profesional*, which amounts to a training for various basic trades if not very bright, or to the institute where they work their way up to the *bacho*, the final school examination and thus to university in one of the major cities.

Salamanca has the reputation of being the best university, much like Oxford or Cambridge, but such a statement will probably be pilloried by those who did not go there. However, whether you have been to Granada, Córdoba, Sevilla or Barcelona is not that important. It's the degree that counts.

# Government

While Franco was alive he tried hard to take a page out of Queen Victoria's book of repression and keep the Spanish people under control but, unlike Queen Victoria with the English, he totally failed to curb the Spanish sense of fun and only managed to make them a trifle unhappy for a number of years.

The day he died, all staid, right-wing papers on the news-stands were immediately replaced by *Playboy* magazine and the beaches went topless.

Between 1982 and 1996 the PSOE (Spanish Socialist Workers' Party) under the Presidency of Felipe González was in power. During this time a great deal was achieved, which was nodded at sagely by the voting public, and a great deal went wrong, which entertained everybody royally for days on end.

First, a judicial enquiry into illegal death squads sent a former Interior Minister, a General and five senior officials to trial for mishandling an anti-terrorist operation.

Next, the Head of the Guardia Civil (the most powerful policeman in the land), his subordinates and several Cabinet Ministers were sent to jail for a magnificent number of serious misdeeds. Then a body of shrewd accountants investigating the collapse of a high street bank discovered that the Chairman had quietly milked fourteen thousand million pesetas (£70 million) during his six years' tenure, using a network of companies controlled in Switzerland to launder the funds.

Not surprisingly, in the March 1996 elections, González's right-wing rival, José Maria Aznar (a former Tax Inspector) and his Partido Popular (PP) was voted into power and the corruption-dazed country sat back for a breather. But not for long.

Within six months, dishonesty reared its head again when a right-wing Cabinet Minister was accused of being involved in yet another shady deal, which the media fanned into a dishonourable soap to keep everyone happy.

Though democracy has taken a firm hold and Spain has made its mark on the international front, joined the European Union, boosted its per capita income and now imports Heinz baked beans, the Constitution which established that there must be solidarity between the regions is a little jittery.

The PP has only 156 deputies in the 350 seat congress and depends on 16 Catalan votes and the support of the Catalan President for success. Jordy Pujol (the said Catalan President) wants co-fiscal responsibility and a great deal more power, so has become a major embarrassment to the Tax Inspector who finds himself on the verge of humiliation whenever he sets out to propose a reform.

While political in-fighting continues and the media keep a vigilant eye open for the mega corruption scandal to end all corruption scandals, the man in the street continues to worry more about what *tapas* he may enjoy for lunch than how his government's future will affect him.

# Bureaucracy

It is impossible to reside in Spain without spending part of your life applying to an authority for some sort of permit, either to be allowed to go on existing once you are born, to be allowed to stay if you have come from abroad, to be allowed to start a business, drive a car, build a house, pull one down or be buried in reasonable comfort.

Several weeks or months should be set aside in the pursuance of obtaining a necessary official permit to do what you want, as essential queuing becomes inevitable.

You will first have to queue for a form applying for the permit, then queue to hand it in once you have filled in all the irrelevant questions asked.

You will then be told that the application is not valid unless presented with two or three other documents which can only be acquired from two or three other departments where you will also have to queue. These departments will be in other office buildings in a different part of the town, or in a different town altogether.

Having successfully collected the necessary papers, you will be informed that the permit you have received is not considered officially effective until it has been stamped by the *jefe* (boss) of yet another department, and he will point out that the law on this particular issue has been changed because of new regulations from Brussels, which will mean that you have to start all over again.

In Spain no two official departments open at the same time, though all are closed in the afternoons.

When starting the arduous battle to procure a permit you should therefore arm yourself with a list of the dates of all national and local feast days, saint's days and holidays, the mayor's birthday, his assistant's wedding anniversary and, if possible, the coffee drinking habits of all minor officials.

Thankfully the Spanish became aware a long time ago of the difficulties put in the way of the average citizen by their civil service, so invented the *gestoría*.

The word *gestor* has many meanings: superintendent, manager, agent, proxy, promoter, representative, attorney, but a *gestoría* (the office of the *gestor*) is the haven to which all desperate permit seekers should run in search of help before losing their minds.

*Gestors* are highly paid go-fers who will charge you the earth for getting all the documents you need to be granted a permit, and they will even get you the permit itself, valid, signed and sealed by the right authority. In this they are always successful since they are either directly related to the heads of civil service departments and have coffee with them every day, or only open their office in the afternoons because in the mornings they run the departments that have caused you all the problems.

# Business

Anyone entering into negotiations with Spanish corporations should arm themselves with great patience and some knowledge of their business methods and conduct.

# Management

Senior executives are usually the sons of the Managing Director, his nephews, or married to the Chairman's daughters. No director will gain respect by asking subordinates or anyone else for their opinion. It is considered a sure sign of weakness and will generate insecurity among the staff. Those in command must not seek advice but take decisions themselves, which is why they are so highly paid.

In big companies, heads of departments are not encouraged to communicate so that they will not interfere with each others' work. Individuals within departments are not encouraged to communicate with each other either, in case they, too, stop minding their own business.

This, of course, negates team spirit (unheard of in Spain anyway) and makes sure that no-one knows what anyone else is doing, which may account for delays of up to five years before letters are answered.

Reprimands or criticisms are only accepted from the very top and on no account will be admitted. No-one is ever wrong. Colleagues are not exactly blamed, but the buck is passed pretty swiftly to another department which will not understand the problem and shelve it for ever.

In most Spanish businesses, family connections, longstanding friendships and loyalty far outweigh cleverness or intelligence. Character and amiability are rated higher than business acumen. And if you are amusing during coffee time, you will get the job.

Ambition in business is rare. The Spanish do not care about success, their main aim in life is to have enough money not to work. Dangling the carrot of promotion with a higher income and more expenses to encourage an employee to move to another area seldom brings positive results.

# Banking and Accountancy

To stop nosy parkers from finding out what a company is up to, no self-respecting business will dream of using just one bank. The concept of only banking at Lloyds or Barclays, or staying loyal to one branch of these, makes no sense to the Spanish at all.

Eggs should be scattered in as many baskets as possible. In this way no-one can find out exactly what is going on, not even the accountants themselves.

Spanish accountancy systems are designed to give the impression that they will enlighten anyone who studies them. They are in fact calculated to conceal all financial information from everyone, especially the Board of Directors and shareholders.

# Meetings

There is no point in arranging meetings as no-one will turn up. In the case of international corporations or companies dealing with exports, meetings are arranged to please foreign management and visiting clients and some people will turn up if coffee is on offer, but no-one will take any notice of what is said as the final decisions are always made by the boss.

# Competitors

Four words should be memorised in connection with comments on individual competitors, clients or colleagues:

*valiente* – a courageous decision maker – he'll probably drop you right in it

*bueno* – a clever dick, but honest with it

*inteligente* – boringly reliable, may well quote unintelligible statistics till the cows come home

*listo* – sharp as they come. Don't trust him for a second.


# Conversation

The Spanish love to talk, so much so that they indulge in *ocio* anytime anywhere, invariably in the middle of the road ignoring the traffic chaos they are causing, or in the supermarket in front of the dairy produce counter resulting in some housewives in a hurry having to go without milk, butter or cheese for the week.

Another aspect of chatting is the *tertulia*, strictly speaking 'an assembly', but generally meaning debate. Usually organised to take place in a café by a group of intellectuals hell bent on airing their views on a burning subject close to their heart, the *tertulia* ends up by being a disorganised gathering of well-oiled individuals all shouting their opinions at each other at the same time unaware that no-one is taking a blind bit of a notice of what they are saying. Not unlike Parliament in Madrid.


## Insults

It takes a few minutes for a Spaniard to decide whether it is worth his while getting annoyed, but once the decision has been made there is no going back.

"*Hijo de puta*!!!" (son of a slag/scrubber/tart/whore) exclaimed with fury and unmatchable indignation will start the flow, after which every imaginable insult will be hurled at the subject which caused the provocation, be it human, animal, vegetable, or mineral.

'*Coño*' (a particular part of a woman's anatomy) is used so much that it has no effect at all, likewise '*joder*' (the slang for sexual intercourse).

On the other hand, suggesting that a person is lacking brains, '*maleducado*' (uneducated/ill-bred) '*imbécil*' (imbecile) or even the mild '*tonto*' (nincompoop) can cause umbrage, and frequently does.


## The Taboo Subject

Few people living outside Spain understand that the Franco regime (1939-1975) had an amazing impact on the foreign media who wrote a great deal about how they saw the Spanish character during those 36 years – proud, xenophobic, nationalistic – because that was the image put out by propaganda. Today the average Spaniard will be found to shrug his shoulders and gaze with some bewilderment at the perpetuation of this image by the pundits.

The bewilderment and the shrugging of the shoulders, which have become part of the Spanish character, originate from what is known as the 'bewildered generation', those who are now in their late sixties and seventies, who were children during the Civil War and had to try to make sense of life in the years that followed it – from internecine strife to Fascism to democracy and a King.

The generation that came after adapted quickly enough to the total liberation the country experienced following Franco's death, but there are still many who remember only too well how their neighbours, or cousins, or even brothers and sisters behaved during the Civil War and cannot forgive, while the children of those people are free from the stilting bitterness.

The subject of the Civil War remains taboo. It is not enjoyable.

# The Author

Drew Launay first went to Spain in 1969 and did not understand the Spanish way of life at all.

He went again in 1972 and understood it even less.

In 1975 he married a fiery, foot-stamping, mad-as-a-sombrero Andalusian and *had* to understand it or die.

Born in London of French parents, given an English education, finished in France, living in Spain and speaking three languages, he is the consummate European: one who finds no difficulty in driving on either the left or right side of the road.

Author of more than a dozen novels written under various pseudonyms and published in Czechoslovakia (that was), Denmark, Germany, Italy, Portugal and Poland, he goes to Rickmansworth for his holidays.

Drew Launay now lives permanently south of Granada, broadcasts on the BBC about Spain and writes books – when not picking olives or curing mountain hams.